P9-APT-654

Jobs People Do

Mail Carriers

by Mary Meinking

PEBBLE
a capstone imprint

Pebble Explore is published by Pebble, an imprint of Capstone.
1710 Roe Crest Drive
North Mankato, Minnesota 56003
www.capstonepub.com

Library of Congress Cataloging-in-Publication Data
Names: Meinking, Mary, author.
Title: Mail carriers / by Mary Meinking.
Description: North Mankato : Pebble, 2020. | Series: Jobs people do | Includes index. | Audience: Ages 6–8. | Summary: "Mail carriers take care of all sorts of mail. Get the inside scoop on what it's like to be a mail carrier. Readers will learn what mail carriers do, the tools they use, and how people get this exciting job"— Provided by publisher.
Identifiers: LCCN 2019052601 (print) | LCCN 2019052602 (ebook) | ISBN 9781977123497 (hardcover) | ISBN 9781977126658 (paperback) | ISBN 9781977123558 (adobe pdf)
Subjects: LCSH: Letter carriers—Juvenile literature.
Classification: LCC HE6241 .M445 2020 (print) | LCC HE6241 (ebook) | DDC 383/.145023—dc23
LC record available at https://lccn.loc.gov/2019052601
LC ebook record available at https://lccn.loc.gov/2019052602

Image Credits
Newscom: KRT/Dan Honda, 27, Reuters/Robert Galbraith, 13, UPI/Tyler Mallory, 11, ZUMA Press/Adolphe Pierre-Louis, 9, ZUMA Press/Alexey Bychkov, 22, ZUMA Press/Andy Abeyta, 21, ZUMA Press/Jack Kurtz, 15, ZUMA Press/Joan Barnett Lee, 7, ZUMA Press/Jose M. Osorio, 6, ZUMA Press/Leonard Ortiz, 18, ZUMA Press/Richard Tsong-Taatarii, 17; Shutterstock: Drazen Zigic, Cover, eddtoro, 4, Johnny Habell, 25, Joseph Sohm, 1, NAE BERG, 14, Vladimirkarp, 23; Wikimedia: Library of Congress, 28

Editorial Credits
Editor: Gena Chester; Designer: Kyle Grenz; Media Researcher: Jo Miller; Production Specialist: Spencer Rosio

All internet sites appearing in back matter were available and accurate when this book was sent to press.

Printed in the United States
PO117

Table of Contents

Words in **bold** are in the glossary.

What Is a Mail Carrier?

A mail carrier slides down an icy street. He is pushing a cart. Snow falls on a mail cart. The holiday season is a busy time for a mail carrier!

Mail carriers used to be called mailmen. Today, about as many women as men deliver mail. Carriers bring mail to homes and offices. They do this almost every day. They work outdoors. They deliver mail in all types of weather.

Mail carriers like helping others. They need to be friendly. They might have to ask people to sign for packages.

Mail carriers must pay attention. They have a lot of mail to deliver. Mail needs to go to the right people.

Carriers must be strong. Their bags and packages are heavy. Some carry the mail from door to door. Others carry carts of letters and boxes.

What Mail Carriers Do

Mail carriers bring people mail. They walk or drive a mail truck. They have **routes**. Routes are paths they always take.

Carriers can pick up letters on their route. A mailbox has a flag up. The carrier looks inside. A new letter needs to be delivered! The carrier takes it to the **post office**. The new mail is sent out.

PCH
Publishers Clearing House

Mail carriers put their mail in bins. The bins are loaded into mail trucks. Carriers drive to each mailbox on their routes.

Some carriers use bags for mail. They walk their routes.

Some people bring packages to post offices. People can also ask carriers to pick up packages at their homes. Carriers take them to a post office. Then the packages are delivered.

UNITED STATES
POSTAL SERVICE
UNITED STATES POSTAL SERVICE
LABEL
OTHER
END
UNITED STATES
POSTAL SERVICE

Where Mail Carriers Work

Mail carriers start their workdays at post offices. Then they go out on their routes. They can work in cities or in the country.

Carriers in big cities fill bags with letters and boxes. They carry the bags from door to door. Some carriers use a cart to carry the mail. Carriers in towns or in the country drive mail trucks.

U.S.MAIL

Mail goes all around the world. But some places are hard to get to.

Some mail carriers bring mail by boat. They go on large lakes and rivers. People have their mailboxes next to the water. Mail boats deliver to large ships too.

Some places in Alaska and Canada have no roads. There, mail comes by plane.

Mail even goes to the Grand Canyon! Mail carriers use mules to get to the bottom. They also deliver food and **supplies**.

How Mail Carriers Help

Mail carriers connect friends and family. They deliver birthday cards. Some bring gifts. They help people stay connected.

Carriers also deliver goods for **companies**. People order things. Carriers make sure people get what they ordered.

The post office is very busy. But the busiest season is the holidays. Most people send cards and gifts. It's important these things get to people in time. Everyone enjoys hearing from loved ones over the holidays.

The post office delivers to people in the **military**. Families can send notes, cards, or food to those serving overseas. Carriers deliver these things for free.

Mail Carriers' Clothes and Tools

Mail carriers wear **uniforms**. When it's hot, they wear short sleeves. Carriers also wear shorts. When it's cold, they bundle up! They wear winter coats. They put on gloves and snow pants. Carriers wear a hat too.

Mail carriers walk a lot. They wear comfy shoes. In winter, they wear boots.

Most carriers drop off mail in mailboxes. Some mailboxes are on the sides of streets. Some are by front doors. Other mail is left at group mailboxes. It has a small box for each home or business. These are locked. Group boxes save time. Carriers can deliver to many people at one stop.

Some packages can't fit in a mailbox. Instead, they can be locked in group mail areas. Or, they can be left at front doors. Sometimes people need to pick up these packages at post offices.

How to Become a Mail Carrier

Mail carriers need to finish high school. They need to be at least 18 years old. They need a driver's license. And, they need to be good drivers.

Future carriers must take a test. If they pass, they can apply for a mail carrier job.

New mail carriers get their own routes. They train on the job. They learn the names of the streets they will drive on. They work with more **experienced** carriers. Then they can work alone. After working many years, they pick which routes they want.